# Great Danes

by Grace Hansen

Abdo DOGS Kids

**abdopublishing.com**

Published by Abdo Kids, a division of ABDO, P.O. Box 398166, Minneapolis, Minnesota 55439.



Printed in China

052016

092016

THIS BOOK CONTAINS RECYCLED MATERIALS

Photo Credits: iStock, Shutterstock, Thinkstock

Production Contributors: Teddy Borth, Jennie Forsberg, Grace Hansen

Design Contributors: Dorothy Toth, Laura Mitchell

Cataloging-in-Publication Data

Names: Hansen, Grace, author.

Title: Great Danes / by Grace Hansen.

Description: Minneapolis, MN : Abdo Kids, [2017] | Series: Dogs. Set 2 | Includes bibliographical references and index.

Identifiers: LCCN 2015959121 | ISBN 9781680805178 (lib. bdg.) | ISBN 9781680805734 (ebook) | ISBN 9781680806298 (Read-to-me ebook)

Subjects: LCSH: Great Dane--Juvenile literature.

Classification: DDC 636.73--dc23

LC record available at http://lccn.loc.gov/2015959121

# Table of Contents

## Great Danes

The Great Dane is one of the tallest dog **breeds**. It can grow nearly 3 feet (1 m) tall!

Everything about the Great Dane is big. It has long legs and a long tail. Its head is very large.

Great Danes have large ears. Some are **cropped**, while others are folded over. Their paws can be as big as human hands!

The Great Dane's body is **muscular**. It is covered in short, shiny hair.

Great Danes come in many colors. They can also have **markings**.

## Care & Exercise

Great Danes shed a lot. Brushing them often will help. An occasional bath is also needed.

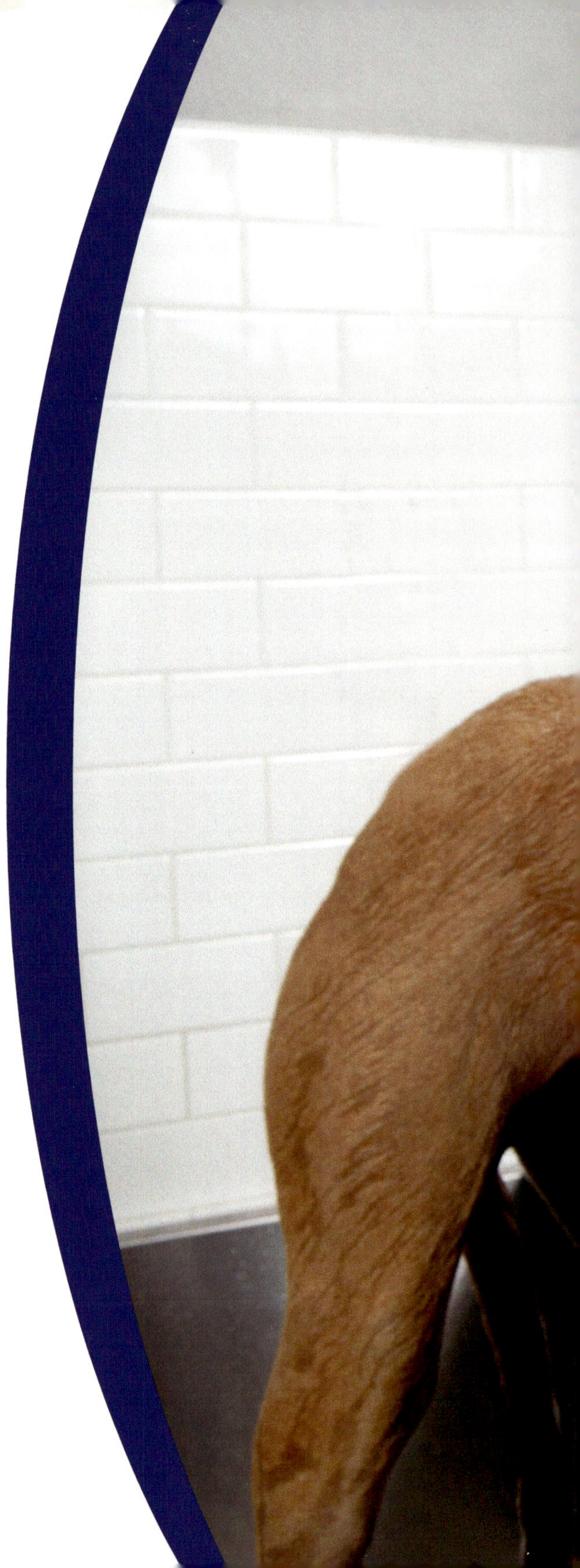

Great Danes do not need a lot of exercise. They'd rather lie on the couch! But, a few walks a day are important.

Great Danes need **high quality** dog food. A raised food bowl is also needed. Proper feeding will keep them healthy!

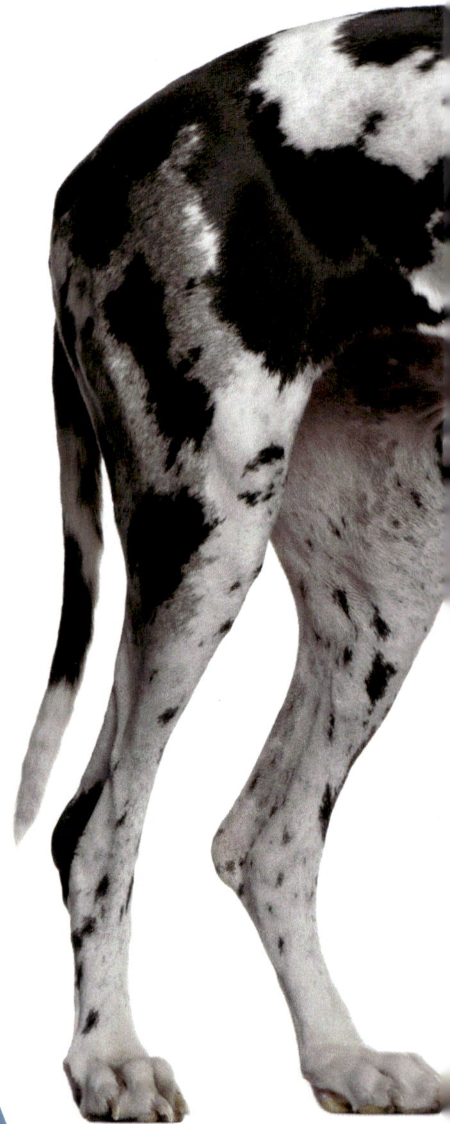

## Gentle Giants

Great Danes can look scary!

But they are very gentle.

They are good with kids.

They are loving members

of their families!

## More Facts

- Great Danes will nudge owners with their big heads when they want attention!
- These big dogs easily get cold. A dog coat is nice for walks in cold winter months.
- Because of its size, the Great Dane has a very short life expectancy. Great Danes usually live between 7.5 and 10 years.

# Glossary

**breed** – a certain kind of dog.

**cropped** – made to stick straight up.

**high quality** – the best.

**marking** – a mark or pattern of marks on an animal's fur.

**muscular** – strong and athletic.

# Index



## abdokids.com

Use this code to log on to abdokids.com and access crafts, games, videos and more!